Matthew D. Hutcheson

Patriot in Prison
In Defense of America

This book resides in the following BISAAC Categories:

- Nonfiction > Political Science > History & Theory
- Nonfiction > Political Science > Comparative Politics

For more about Matthew D. Hutcheson, and other writings, visit www.bellohutch.com

In Latin, "Bello" means "fight for."
BelloHutch@gmail.com

AreULost Press

For more information:

info@areulost.org

Table of Contents

Foreword

Will America be Ok?

It is a question on many people's minds today.

In that special comforting way for which Matthew D. Hutcheson has come to be known, he not only answers the question, "*Will America be Ok?*" in the affirmative, but he also provides desperately needed insight and comfort to a nation groaning under the stress and weight of political strife.

In Defense of America clears away the fog of confusion which has settled upon America's younger generations. Is America evil? What about its founders? Were they evil? Will America survive?

Matthew helps the reader understand why America is truly exceptional and why the *Stars and Stripes* shall forever wave. He shares memorialized conversations with young inmates who ultimately come to understand why they should love America and continue to believe in her.

In many ways, Matthew D. Hutcheson is like a modern-day Dean Alfange, the late, skilled politician who wrote the award-winning essay, *An American Creed* in the 1950s.

The essay originally appeared in <u>This Week Magazine</u>. Several years later the essay was published in <u>Reader's Digest</u> in the October, 1952 issue, and once again in the January, 1954 issue. The Freedoms

Foundation at Valley Forge gave Alfange an award for the composition in 1952.

Here is Alfanges' essay:

"I do not choose to be a common man. It is my right to be uncommon. I seek to develop whatever talents God gave me—not security. I do not wish to be a kept citizen, humbled and dulled by having the state look after me. I want to take the calculated risk; to dream and to build, to fail and to succeed. I refuse to barter incentive for a dole. I prefer the challenges of life to the guaranteed existence; the thrill of fulfillment to the stale calm of utopia. I will not trade freedom for beneficence nor my dignity for a handout. I will never cower before any earthly master nor bend to any threat. It is my heritage to stand erect, proud and unafraid; to think and act myself, enjoy the benefit of my creations and to face the world boldly and say – 'This, with God's help, I have done.' All this is what it means to be an American."

It is as though those words were spoken by Matthew D. Hutcheson in the first instance. You will see that Alfange's words apply to Hutcheson as they do to himself.

The contents of this small book have had a profound and life-changing impact on the lives of many.

I believe it will likewise change your life and that of your loved ones.

Lee Ofner, DDS

Prologue

Patriot in Prison

In Defense of America

Testifying Before Congress 2007

The pages you are about to read were written by Matthew D. Hutcheson, under the extreme conditions of federal prison, between June 11, 2017 and July 6, 2019. These writings include updates from prison to Matthew's family and friends memorializing experiences and conversations. Each memorialization was written without source materials and has been edited and converted from emails by Jay Inman, Lt. Colonel, US ARMY (Ret.).

Testifying Before Congress 2010

This prisoner-sourced document is part of a soon to be published book entitled, *Patriot in Prison*, which we believe will be one of the most important explanations of liberty and America you will ever read.

Respectfully Submitted,

Jerry L. Melchisedeck, Sr., Lt Col USAF (Ret).
Jay Inman, Lt Col US Army (Ret).
Robert Gilbeau, Fmr. Rear Admiral US Navy (Ret).
Lee Ofner, DDS
John Jenkins, JD

Chapter 1

The American Hypothesis
September 25, 2019
© Matthew D. Hutcheson 2017-2019

The following inspiring message was originally written June 11, 2017 by Matthew D. Hutcheson, then incarcerated at FCI-Lompoc, as an email to his family.

POSTED September 25, 2019 to Microsoft's® Education Blog

***

There are two local colleges here (I think both are out of Santa Barbara) which offer Associate degrees in a variety of subjects. The classes are usually full. In prison, every societal and cultural status is represented. There are rich and poor. There are educated and ignorant. There are the English proficient and the "just learning." There are Asians, Europeans, Africans, South Americans, Eskimos, Polynesians, and everyone in between. The entire continuum is represented in the classes of the local colleges.

One young man I met soon after I arrived here is Vietnamese. He goes by "John" and one of the classes he is taking is "American History 118."

He and I have become friends, but as you can imagine, language is a barrier. When coupled with a lack of knowledge of American History with which most of us grew up, it makes for a very stressful time for him in class.

The visiting professor ("Professor Barker") gave the American History class an assignment. I paraphrase John's understanding of the assignment:

"GIVEN THE POLITICAL UNREST IN THE UNITED STATES, IN LIGHT OF A VERY ACRIMONIOUS ELECTION, AND IN A SEEMINGLY CHAOTIC CHANGE IN ADMINISTRATIONS, AND IN ALL OF THE INTERNATIONAL WARS AND FINANCIAL INSTABILITY AT HOME AND ABROAD, PLEASE DEVELOP A REASONABLE HYPOTHESIS FOR THE FUTURE OF AMERICA."

My friend John was overwhelmed with this assignment. He did not have a clue what to write. So, he hunted down his buddy "Hutch" and asked for some help.

He and I worked on it together. Here is John's finished paper:

***

If it is true that history repeats itself, then it is a plausible hypothesis that some (or perhaps all) of the historical scenarios considered in this course will occur again, in some form, in our immediate or long-term future. However, that thought is not the central idea in support of this short paper. My hypothesis revolves around a slightly different premise as follows:

"The social, financial, and economic forces that shape today's America are no different from those which have worked to impact the America of our past."

Using this basic premise as my starting point, we find ourselves confronted with some largely general questions about what it is to be an American – and whether or not our collective perception of the "American Experience" has changed significantly over time. But more specifically (and more to the point of this paper), we might approach the subject of American History by asking another, yet more subtle question:

"If the historical forces affecting America have at times been variable, then what constant of the 'American Experience' has allowed us to persist?"

I believe, as many others do, that it is the robust nature of the United States Constitution – more than anything else – which has acted to propel America forward and to ensure her dynamic progress. The United States Constitution anchors Americans, one and all, to a unique and unalienable set of principles; principles that serve to hold up our enduring national ideology – principles which are far superior to those of any other civilized nation.

But, what do I have for proof, you may ask? Well, as with so many other points, the measure of a nation's greatness is often gauged by its finances. The United States, for example, leads the entire world in its steady and lavish production of gross domestic product – overmatching every competing country by an order of several magnitudes at least – including the out-producing of China by many, many trillions of dollars annually. Whether we attribute these facts to Divine

Acts of Providence, or to the simple goodness of our founding principles (which are also given through Divine Providence), one point is absolutely certain: America not only persists through conflict, she seems to thrive upon it.

However, you may ask, "Are we not living in especially dangerous times? Is the country not in an absolute state of peril, more so than at any other time in history?" Well, frankly, the answer to that question, is "no, not really." The America of today, if truth be told, is in no worse shape than she was ten, twenty, or even one hundred years ago. She is stronger and actually improving. Here is why:

We nearly lost the Revolutionary War when on at least two separate occasions were it not for rogue winter storms which wrecked the Redcoats' visibility in one instance and drove back their boats and warships in another. The Civil War was also nearly lost but for the Confederacy having misplaced its battle plans and strategic documents in an abandoned tent, later to be found by a Union scout.

These events are not luck. They are caused by a Being, more intelligent than, and superior to, us. We then conclude that this Supremely Intelligent and Benevolent Being wants America to exist and go on existing.

It might surprise most readers to know that America's destiny has been absolutely littered by an almost bizarre series of impossibly close-calls, extending far beyond those of our Revolutionary and Civil Wars. Further examples include the United States' narrowly winning the race against Germany to construct World War II's first atomic bomb – and in the 11th hour to break the enigma code.

It is not the point of this short paper to showcase America's propensity for running a tight race – although she has done just that. The point here is to highlight America's iron-clad perseverance, which when considered in its proper historical context, has been absolutely miraculous.

So, what does history have to say, overall, about America? Is she good? Is she bad? Does Manifest Destiny actually exist, or was it all just a bit of excessive exuberance coupled with the coincidences and circumstances of the day? If we could pick just one universal trait to define our nation, what might that trait be? Although this last question is a tough one, to be sure, our Nation has existed for long enough for us to have a good look at her pedigree – and she is, by all accounts, unique.

History has shown us, time and time again, that America's people are a diverse and complicated bunch. We are a multi-talented tapestry of enormous untapped potential – quietly surging, nearly glowing – as we bend and sway against the political and economic wind gusts of the day.

It is precisely these qualities, a sense of unpredictability tempered with hope, which has somehow been infused into our Constitution – and is embodied there – stamping its manifest presence onto our destiny. Thus ordained, America has led us over, or through, almost every imaginable obstacle, surviving both reformation and greed, revolution and war – and as always, we will persist, we will adapt, we will prevail. America always will. It is the American Hypothesis.

This article can be found online at:

<https://education.microsoft.com/Story/CommunityTopic?token=McNxl>

Chapter 2

Independence Day 2019
In Defense of America
July 6, 2019
© Matthew D. Hutcheson 2019

Introduction by Dr. Lee Ofner:

Good Evening, All, and Happy Independence Day,

We have so much for which to be thankful. I have spoken frequently about my friend, Matt, who is incarcerated in federal prison in Littleton, CO. Matt is imprisoned on false charges and is guilty of nothing. Hopefully, justice will prevail soon and he will then experience his freedom again. Please understand that Matt is not bitter. Matt is one of the most optimistic and joyful people I have ever known. Even considering what the government, US Attorneys, prosecutors, etc, have done to Matt, he is a true patriot. Matt holds no grudges, he loves America. You can read it in his writing. Below, I have included a conversation Matt had with a fellow inmate earlier this week. Please feel free to share with anyone who may be inspired by his thoughts. I found this interchange to be very enlightening. There are revelations that I never knew. Among other talents, Matt is truly an educator, too. Please enjoy and I would love to hear your feedback. Thank you.

Dr Lee Ofner

719-337-1660

Lee@leeofner.com

***

Dear Fam,

Happy Independence Day!

I love America! I always have.

Since I have been in prison, I have grown to love her even more.

This July 4, I am going to recount a conversation I had with a 30-year-old about America and his misunderstanding about her. He has been "indoctrinated" with anti-American poison and I hope the conversation helped clear some things up with him. By the way, prison is a breeding ground for every lie about America you can think of. (Hint to society: eliminate the breeding ground of those lies! I also recommend reading chapter 33 of Quinny. www.quinnythebook.com.)

Here is how the conversation went:

Young Man: "I hate America. When I am released, I am going to leave the United States and never come back!"

Me: Silence for a moment, and then: "It is too bad. But I guess it is best because America needs people who will produce results for society by providing stability, building trust with friends, family, and neighbors; those with whom you come in contact should never fear for their safety or well-being because you are around. Society expects every member to use his or her talents to produce goods or offer services which make peoples' lives better. You are right. You are unable to do any of it, so it is best that you leave."

Young Man: "What the? Just who do you think you..."

[He stopped for a moment and considered his reaction. If he hates America so much, why does he even care what I said? The truth is, he loves her, too! Everyone does! There is a reason. America loves us! She gives us freedom. In the words of Daniel J. Boorstin, "Freedom means the opportunity to be what we never thought we would be." Freedom alone makes things better than any government ever could. It is not the U.S. government which makes America great; it is the liberty the government is tasked to preserve which makes her great. Protecting liberty for its citizens is the government's PRIMARY legitimate function.]

Me: "Yes, go ahead with your thought."

Young Man: "Our nation was founded upon the evils of slavery. The founding fathers were evil. Thomas Jefferson was a rapist. He raped his slave, Sally Hemmings."

Me: "Who gave you that information?"

Young Man: "One of my professors from college. I'm not stupid. I went to college and have a degree."

Me: "I commend you for that education. Good for you. Your professor told you an untruth. Sorry."

Young Man: "Are you calling my professor a liar?"

Me: "Yes."

Young Man: "You are a [explicative]."

Me: "Sorry you feel that way, but your professor's low self-esteem is manifesting as anger towards America. He does not really hate America. He hates himself or his life and projects it on America."

Young Man: Silence.

Me: "Our founding fathers were great men. Very few men today can even scratch the surface of the depth of their character, bravery, and moral excellence. They were not racists. Thomas Jefferson was not a rapist."

Young Man: "You are so full of [explicative]! You don't know."

Me: "Well, if I do not know, then neither do you. Mr. college, you just caught yourself in a logical contradiction. You realize it, right? Look, let us have a conversation. You do not need to curse at me every time I say something with which you disagree. How about we have an intellectual conversation, like two dignified men? The more persuasive argument will be the one we both embrace. Fair enough?"

Young Man: "I'm going to roast your [explicative]!"

Me: "No swearing!"

Young Man: "Sorry."

Me: "Ok then. Let us talk about slavery. It is a terrible thing. The founding fathers were horrified by it."

Young Man: "No they weren't! They loved it! They were slave owners!"

Me: "Being slave owners was an unfortunate reality of their day. It does not mean they loved owning other human beings."

Young Man: "Prove it."

Me: "Take George Washington for example. In 1786 he wrote a letter to Robert Morse, saying: 'There is not a man living who wishes more sincerely than I do to see a plan adopted for the abolishment of slavery.'"

Young Man: "I've never heard that before."

Me: "It is part of American history. The letter is available for anyone to read with a little research."

Young Man: "Then why did Washington have slaves?"

Me: "Like I said, it was the reality of their day. But they did not agree with it. Many founding fathers worried that if they freed their slaves, they would somehow end up re-enslaved with cruel and violent slave masters. Taking care of them and providing for them was the best they could do under the circumstances. There just was not an easy way to deal with the issue quickly. Those realities were harsh of life at that time. It was not until 1863 that slavery was finally abolished. It costs hundreds of thousands of American lives. Americans took the slavery issue very seriously then and we take it seriously now."

Young Man: "But what about Jefferson?"

Me: "Jefferson wrote the Declaration of Independence."

Young Man: "Right, I know that."

Me: "I know you do. What most people do not know is that in the first edition of the Declaration which was proposed at the Second Continental Congress, it said something like: 'King George waged cruel war against the life and liberty of a distant people (African slaves) who never offended him, capturing and carrying them into slavery in another hemisphere or to incur miserable death in their transportation. The King of Great Britain determined to keep open a slave market in which men should be bought and sold.' Thomas Jefferson called it the 'execrable commerce.'"

Young Man: "That's not in the Declaration of Independence!"

Me: "Not anymore. But it was in the original version presented to the Continental Congress. Jefferson was forced to take it out when South Carolina and Georgia threatened to walk out of the Continental Congress unless that paragraph was removed. A sad but necessary compromise was made so that South Carolina and Georgia would remain part of the fight for liberty and independence. The Colonies would not have won the Revolutionary War without them."

Young Man: "A little ironic, don't you think, that slaves were the bargaining chip that saved the Colonies and made America possible?"

Me: "It is inspiring that the slaves enabled America to win, and by so doing, the slaves ultimately won their freedom for their posterity. It is one of the greatest comeback stories in the history of the world. Keep in mind, white men did not invent slavery. The slave trade goes back millennia. However, even more recently Muslim pirates from Morocco, Algeria, Tunisia, and Libya (from the sixteenth to the early nineteenth century) captured over one million white Europeans and sold them into Muslim nations as slaves. No one talks about it. Thomas Jefferson's autobiography (1821) said, 'Nothing is more certainly written in the book of fate than that the slaves are to be free.' It does not sound like someone who wants the slaves to remain slaves."

Young Man: "He really said that?"

Me: "Yes he did. You can look it up yourself. It is part of American history. It is only fair to put it into proper perspective. A scant 74 years passed from the time the United States became a sovereign nation in 1789 until slavery was finally abolished in 1863, which is extremely rapid social change for something of such a magnitude of importance, even for our day. It is yet another example of America's moral exceptionalism in light of the nearly 300 years of slavery presided over by British rule which preceded it.

Young Man: "But he raped his slave, Sally Hemmings."

Me: Taking in a big breath and sighing loudly. "Thomas Jefferson's wife was named Martha, just like George Washington's wife."

Young Man: "Interesting. I didn't know that."

Me: "Well, Martha Jefferson's father took a second wife of sorts – perhaps more aptly called a 'concubine.' Anyway, Martha's father had six children with his 'concubine.' Sally Hemmings was number six."

Young Man: [Jaw dropping]

Me: "You see, Martha Jefferson and Sally Hemmings were half-sisters. After Martha Jefferson died, Hemmings visited Jefferson in Paris while he was Ambassador to France. It was there that Hemmings and Jefferson fell in love. In the law of Moses, men married the wives of their deceased brothers. Back then, it could easily mean marrying sisters. Jefferson knew Hemmings was Martha Jefferson's half-sister; he saw her and treated her that way. He loved her. She loved him. They did not marry; they probably could not under the laws that prevailed at the time, but Jefferson might have married her upon his return from France if Virginia law had permitted it. It is telling that Hemmings could have stayed in Paris in 1789 as a free woman but instead returned home with Jefferson because she loved him. He was no rapist. They had a relationship."

Young Man: [Stunned. Unable to respond.]

Me: "Even after Jefferson's death, Hemmings could have written down her story about how he 'mistreated her' if he actually had. Not one slave at Monticello ever even suspected there was anything but love and respect between them or they, too, would have spoken out about it. Jefferson had children with Hemmings. He could have easily sold them at birth to new slave owners if he were ashamed of them and wanted to hide the relationship, but he did not. He loved them."

Young Man: "Then where did all of those rumors come from?"

Me: "A fellow by the name of James Callendar was a journalist who did some work for Jefferson. He, at some point, wanted to become the postmaster for Richmond, Virginia. He approached Jefferson to ask him to use his influence to help him obtain the job, but Jefferson refused to use his influence in that way. Callendar was infuriated and spent the rest of his life making Jefferson's life miserable. The 'rest of his life' was only a year, though. While drunk, Callendar fell off a bridge into a few feet of water and drowned. He was too drunk to stand up. Anyway, all of the negative 'Sally Hemmings' rumors about rape and mistreatment started with that scoundrel, Callendar."

Young Man: "I had no idea."

Me: "Thomas Jefferson really was all the man we hold him to be. He was the 'apostle of democracy,' and the 'oracle of liberty.' What your professor told you was merely to recruit more members to the 'Holy Order of Perpetual Offense.' That term is not mine. I read it somewhere. But it is what professors are doing...they loathe their own lives, so they are recruiting others to join them in their perpetual state of offense. It is that simple."

Young Man: "You know, I'm starting to look at things differently."

Me: "America *can* claim moral superiority over all other nations. It has the power to destroy ALL OTHER nations or assume control over them right now, but it does not. America is virtuous and benevolent. It provides economic relief to over 100 nations. Americans are the most generous people on earth. We produce the most. We create new things. We innovate and experiment. We find cures to diseases and share them with the world. We have revolutionized communications, travel, medical advancements, food production, water distribution, and more. All of those things originated here in America. Almighty God ordained our founding fathers to make it possible. You see, nothing makes a man's thoughts more sharp than when he is under the threat of life or death. The belief that America could ultimately be what it is today, threatened to deliver death to the founding fathers and their families, yet they persisted and prevailed. They were good men of excellent, superior moral virtue. Yes, they were human, and they made mistakes. In balance, when compared to all other great men throughout history, they measure out as the greatest who ever lived."

Young Man: "That actually sounds true. I believe you. But what about socialism? Several professors told me that socialism is necessary for America's future."

Me: "That position is ridiculous. Socialism is a man-made construct. Capitalism, on the other hand, is naturally occurring. We can talk about the difference between the two some other time. For now, I will say...there have been few on earth who understood the evils of socialism more than Great Britain's Winston Churchill, who said, 'Socialism is a philosophy of failure, the creed of ignorance, and the gospel of envy, its inherent virtue is the equal sharing of misery'."

Young Man: "Wow. That is an impressive quote."

Me: "Guess who Mr. Churchill (and all Europeans) can thank for surviving World War II to be able to make such a profound statement? The Americans."

Young Man: "I apologize for being such an [explicative] to you earlier."

Me: "No swearing!"

Young Man: "Sorry. I see now. Our founding fathers were great and they deserve the pedestal history has put them on."

Me: "Thank you for saying so. They were great. America is great. We are a great, loving, generous, compassionate, creative, hardworking people. Why is America the greatest nation on earth? Why is it exceptional? It is simple. America enables her people to produce RESULTS."

***

The young man shook my hand and seemed relieved to be American.

I hope he always remembers.

I conclude these thoughts by sharing an excerpt from an article a friend mailed to me from the Colorado

Springs Gazette. It is a partial quote by deceased politician, Dean Alfange:

"I will not trade my freedom for beneficence nor my dignity for a handout. I will never cower before any earthly master nor bend to any threat. It is my heritage to stand erect, proud and unafraid; to think and act myself, enjoy the benefit of my creations and to face the world boldly and say – 'This, with God's help, I have done.' All this is what it is to be an American."

It is as though those words were spoken by me in the first instance.

God Bless the United States of America.

Life in the Extreme,

Matt

***

Matthew D. Hutcheson may be contacted through regular mail:

Matthew D. Hutcheson
14620-023
FCI Englewood
Satellite Camp
9595 West Quincy Avenue
Littleton, CO 80123

***

For those of you interested in some source material, you will enjoy the following:

Henry Wiencek's Master of The Mountain: Thomas Jefferson & His Slaves, Chapter 1, Farrar Straus & Giroux, 2012, (Kindle location 260-272.

The Women Jefferson Loved by Virginia Scharff, Thomas Jefferson: The Revolution of Ideas by R.B. Bernstein.

Christian Slaves, Muslim Masters: White Slavery in the Mediterranean, the Barbary Coast and Italy, 1500-1800 (Palgrave Macmillan, 2003).

"Major Events in The Jefferson-Hemings Controversy", Lehigh University Digital Library, 2012, (http://digital.lib.lehigh.edu/trial/jefferson/time/).
See also "Sexual Liberties of Thomas Jefferson" by John L. Smith Jr., Journal of The American Revolution, April 18th 2016.

Annette Gordon-Reed's Thomas Jefferson & Sally Hemings: An American Controversy, Chapter 5, University of Virginia Press, Second edition. 1999.

Peter Onuf, Jeffersonian Legacies, "Those Who Labor For My Happiness", Pg. 158, University of Virginia Press, 1993.

Letter from Martha Jefferson Randolph to Thomas Jefferson, November 30th, 1804.

Race Hochdorf,
https://areomagazine.com/2017/09/07/thomas-jefferson-his-enemies

***

5 thoughts on "Independence Day 2019 – In Defense of America" (Online comment)

John Jenkins says:

July 9, 2019 at 9:26 am

I commend you Matthew. This is definitely an eye opener. After listening through viewing your words I could really see and remember through movies and stories from family members who were Freedom

Riders and knew first hand that the fact is there were many slave owners who were not happy about owning slaves but did own slaves and protected them. It's just an unfortunate situation that is in history.

We really do have many unfortunate situations that happen today and all we can do is stay prayed up and always seek a better path than before.

Chapter 3

This article can be found online at:
http://bellohutch.com/independence-day-2019-in-defense-of-america/

***

A 2017 Independence Day message written by Matthew D. Hutcheson to family and friends while at FTC - Oklahoma in transit to FCI - La Tuna then on to FCI - Englewood, Colorado. This message affected the lives of dozens of inmates who had never heard anything like it then, and probably have not heard anything like it since. It has inspired other patriotic articles.

Update July 4, 2017

Four Principles that Will Change Your Lives Forever

© Matthew D. Hutcheson 2019

Oklahoma City, OK

Arriving at Victorville for the third time in around sixteen months was strange.

The third time was less frightening. I had done it before and everything was fine.

I was placed in a cell I had been in before. I had a decent mattress and interesting bunkies. Other than a fist fight in the yard, which was quickly contained, not much happened at Victorville on my third stay.

After around two weeks, at 4 AM I was again instructed to pack up to leave. Once we boarded the bus, a fight broke in the front row seats. Even though those guys were shackled, they still were able to throw elbows, head butts, and gouge with fingers. That fight was also broken up relatively quickly and the two inmates, with shirts torn and bloody, were escorted off the bus.

I just shook my head in disgust. There are some people who are violent before they come to prison. But most violent inmates become that way AFTER being in prison. Some have to fight to survive. It is so sad.

The ride from Victorville to Orange County Airport was uneventful. I admit that I am not 100% certain it was Orange County Airport - I heard someone say it was - so I am repeating here what I heard. The airport was not a large airport. It looked like a municipal airport with some commercial activity. In any event, our bus drove onto the tarmac. There were seven large buses waiting. Shortly the white Boeing 737 arrived with no other identifying markings other than a small round Department of Justice seal near the door and numbers on the tail.

The door opened and a frail internal aluminum auto-fold stairway was deployed from a compartment under the door. Inmates began to deplane. They waited on the tarmac for 10-15 minutes while we exited the buses and were loaded on the plane. We then could see the inmates on the tarmac entering the buses which we had just left. In all, there were over 100 inmates being exchanged.

Once the airplane door closed, we were instructed to put the window shade down. I wondered for what reason. It could be any number of things, obviously all security related. Shortly, we were airborne, and I was, frankly, thrilled to experience the feeling of motion, gravity, speed, bumps, etc., again.

I dozed off for a while and then awakened when I felt the airplane's speed decrease in preparation for landing. Out the window I could see flat fields of grass and oak trees as far as the eye could see. "Where on earth was I?" I wondered.

It looked like Texas. Perhaps it was Oklahoma? The landing was really rough and once on the runway with brakes and engine reversers engaged, the airplane vibrated so severely that it made me very uncomfortable. Never have I felt that kind of vibration on any other flight I have ever been on.

We sat on the airplane, in the summer heat, without water, for a very long time. Inmates were screaming for water. The U.S. Marshals would not provide any. They said they were off the clock now and they were waiting for their relief shift to arrive, so no water until then. "What does shift change have to do with basic humanity?" I thought.

After some number of hours, we were escorted off the airplane onto a sky bridge that was part of the prison itself. We were at the BOP Oklahoma transfer station. The transfer station is a 5-story high mega-prison-complex which can hold thousands of inmates. Hundreds come and go each week.

After waiting on benches in the sky bridge, we were eventually unshackled (keep in mind, it is probably 8 PM by this point and I have been shackled since 6 AM).

My hands and feet were swollen and in excruciating pain. I was so dehydrated I could not speak to answer basic questions asked of me. Once unshackled, we were placed in a holding tank. We were given a lunch sack with bologna, some cookies, and an apple, but still no water.

The guard said, "If you need a drink, get it out of the drinking fountain on the toilet."

As part of the stainless-steel wash basin apparatus, a button can be pushed which sends the water upward like a drinking fountain - or it is what is supposed to happen. I pushed the button, but the water pressure was so low that only a dribble came out. I had to take my plastic bologna bag and fill it with water from the dribble because there was no way I was going to put my mouth down there to drink - especially given all of the vomit already in the sink. I complained to the guards about the conditions and they told me to "zip it or go to the SHU."

Gladly, I zipped it!

After several more hours in the holding tank, we were taken to R&D. Same drill. New clothes. The "interview." Medical in-take forms, etc. Then, we were given a laundry bag with our bedding and we began to be escorted to our respective units.

I was placed on the 5th floor, unit A. It was called "5A." By the time we arrived at our cells, it was around midnight. I immediately started filling my cup in the cell sink and drank and drank and drank until I thought my stomach would burst.

I made my bed and drifted off to sleep. I was exhausted and in much pain.

My muscles were cramping due to dehydration and also due to the awkward position of being shackled for so long. After a while, I was able to gain control over my muscles through techniques I had learned in the Terminal Island SHU. Breathing. Slowing my heart rate. Go into the zone. Off to sleep I went.

The following morning the door opened at 5:45'ish. All of the inmates lined up for their breakfast trays. Cold cereal. Milk. Fruit. After I ate, I emailed Annette. She had already seen from the BOP website that I had been transferred to Oklahoma. An email from her was waiting for me. Her email, in essence, said, "Oklahoma?? What on earth is going on??" By reply, I informed her that I was being sent to La Tuna, El Paso, Texas.

In my email to Annette, I gave her a summary of previous 24 hours. She, and many of you, launched an initiative with my two beloved Senators to have me re-designated to the closer FCI Englewood, Colorado, so my family could more easily visit.

The Oklahoma facility had two tiers of cells like Victorville, but instead of a single TV in the common area, there were four different TV rooms for the various races.

The white TV room was in a covered outside area with no air conditioning. It was in the outside area in which all inmates exercised. Think of it as a large carport. Two sides of the "carport" were cinder blocks painted rusty brown which rose from the slick polished cement floor to a corrugated metal ceiling about 20 feet above. One side were windows that looked back into the common area of the unit.

The telephones and email stations could be seen, along with all of the cells, through the windowed side. The fourth side was enclosed in large gauge wire fencing. Birds flew in and out of the fencing. Several bird families lived in the steel rafter beams of the "carport." It was hot and muggy, just like Texas felt. The outside Oklahoma air was indiscernible from what I remembered Texas air smelling like. Thick. Hot. Grass. Wildflowers. It was July.

There was nothing to do in Oklahoma except sleep, read, watch TV, and do burpees in the "carport." Many inmates would gather around lunchroom tables in the unit at which inmates eat meals, to talk and play cards. It did not take long for a group of inmates to start peppering me with questions.

"You standout like sore thumb. What's your story?" said one inmate.

"I am coming from Lompoc. There was a riot there a few weeks back," I said.

"How long were you at Lompoc?"

"Since December 2016."

"Six months?"

"Yes, about right."

"Where were you before that?"

"Safford, Arizona."

"How long were you there?"

"About eight months."

"What? They've got you on diesel therapy. Why?"

"Good question. Every time I have a hard court filing deadline, I am suddenly moved."

"Man, they are doing you dirty, bro! They're trying to prevent you from beating them, by keeping your legal files in transit. We've seen that before," as the small group nodded their heads in acknowledgment.

I nodded back.

They continued, "We noticed you. You don't look like a sex offender. You have a dignified, educated look about you. You don't look like a drug dealer because you have all of your teeth and have no tattoos. So, you must have been a banker or CEO. Are we close?"

"Yes, sort of, my case is white collar."

"We knew it!"

One of the guys told me he was a former Olympic skier. He was the second Olympian I had met in prison. He was tangled up in selling drugs and his whole life - an excellent heroic American life - suddenly ended in tragedy.

The other fellows told me about their situations, too. Some tragic. Others, ordinary. Some simple crime-equals-punishment scenarios.

One of the inmates was a bona fide wise guy, a gangster associated with the mob. I was struck by how well he spoke, eloquently and persuasively, a skill he no doubt honed from a life on the streets.

One of the guys mentioned he had just come from Terminal Island. I asked him, "Do you know so-and-so?"

"Yes! I sure do!" he said.

I said, "he and I were friends. I heard he had been in the SHU, too."

"He was in the SHU for about four months for some bogus, made-up charge. Hey, wait a minute! I just realized who you are! You're HUTCH! Everyone talked about you at TI. You were in the SHU for made-up charges, too!"

Everyone stared at me. Waiting for a reply.

"Yep, I am Hutch."

"I can't believe it! No way!" He exclaimed in excitement.

Curiosity got the best of more guys as they overheard the excited tone of the conversation. They came and sat down to join in.

The inmate from TI continued, "you were some type of politician, right?"

"Well, not exactly. I was not an elected official. I was a policy advisor to the United States House and Senate on financial markets. My work with Congress encompassed pensions, banking, insurance, and labor - meaning job preservation and/or creation."

"Did you help them write bills?"

"Yep, I sure did, more than one."

"That is incredible! Were you ever on TV?"

"Yes, more than once. Nightly news, C-SPAN, Bloomberg TV."

Silence, the guys were soaking it all in.

One inmate said, "someone told me our nation is not a democracy. I always thought the United States was a democracy."

"Our form of government is a 'republic,'" I replied. "You know what 'the public' is, right? You, our families, me...citizens of the United States."

"Yes, we know what the public is."

"Well, a republic is a 'Represented Public.' We have a government in which the public is represented by officers whom we elect from each state, to represent the citizens of that state in Washington D.C."

"Oh, I see! If you put the 'RE' in '[re]presented,' and add it to 'public,' you get REPUBLIC!"

"Yes, it is a great way to understand what it means. But the word 'respublica' is Latin. 'Res' means 'thing' and 'publica' means 'of the people.' So, republic literally means, 'a thing of the people,' or more precisely, 'a government by the people,' or more aptly, 'we the people!'"

"Whoa, that is awesome! So what does 'democracy' mean?"

"The word 'democracy' is Greek. It consists of two words. The first is 'demos,' which, like the Latin 'publica,' means 'people' or 'public.' You have heard of 'demographics?' That word uses the root 'demos,' too. Demographics is the measurement and analysis of groups of public/people."

"Oh, cool!" one inmate said.

"The second part is 'kratos' which means 'to rule.' If you put 'demos' and 'kratos' together, you have 'demoskratos,' which means 'rule by the people' versus, in contrast to, for example, being ruled by a king."

"Dude, that is incredible! Why haven't we heard any of this information before now?"

"Understanding the meaning of those words really IS neat!" I continued, "so, the Latin word 'respublica' and the Greek word, 'demoskratos,' have very similar meanings. 'rule by the people' or 'we the people.'"

"But I still don't understand the difference if the meanings are essentially the same. So, if the United States is a republic, then what is a democracy? Is there any difference? I'm confused."

"Please forgive me. I did not fully answer your earlier question about a democracy. A true democracy involves citizen input on every decision. In other words, a pure democracy would require every citizen to vote on each and every public policy proposal. Can you imagine having to vote every day on multiple issues? It is just not practical for citizens who have their lives to live. So, we hire a 'Congress' to represent us, hence the republic."

One inmate spoke up and said, "What is the difference between a democrat and a republican?"

"I am glad you asked."

(I should note that just because most of these guys were not formally educated, they were still very intelligent and curious. It made for a very interesting conversation.)

Continuing, I said, "neither political party is perfect. Both have a tendency to become caught up in pursuing their 'personal hobby-horses' which are not in society's best interest. Believe it or not, both parties actually agree on many of the most important things. But the central ideological differences between the two are these:

"**DEMOCRATS** think you cannot take care of yourself and that government is needed to play a 'surrogate parent' to you. In other words, you cannot find a job, you cannot feed your family, you are unable to maintain a permanent spousal relationship, and your children are going to become addicts. It is how democrats think and believe. That belief system is called 'Liberalism' because democrats believe that traditional beliefs and principles are too restrictive and 'liberal' beliefs and behaviors are ok for the individual, even though such behaviors are destructive to society. If liberal behaviors by individuals destroy traditional societal norms, the democrats will hopefully be there to take over.

"**REPUBLICANS** on the other hand think you, and only you, should take care of yourself/your nuclear family, and that government's role is to make sure no one interferes with your ability to do so. If you find yourself in trouble, it is your nuclear family which should be first to step up to assist. That belief system is called 'Conservatism' because republicans hope to preserve/conserve those principles which enable a family to pursue happiness, as stated in the Declaration of Independence, because those principles are best for both the individual and society."

I continued, "of course, both parties have both good and bad qualities which extend beyond the central beliefs that I just explained. Neither is completely good nor completely bad. But political parties can end up politically irrelevant, and the democrats are on the verge of it now. If the republicans do not strictly adhere to correct principles, they, too, could end up politically irrelevant in the future."

One inmate asked, "What is a nuclear family? Like Kim Jong Un and his offspring?" (Laughter.)

"Very clever! But, no, it is not what it means. The nuclear family is a father, mother, and children."

"I never knew my father," said one inmate.

"Neither did I," said another.

"I am very sorry to hear it. The breakdown of the family is what gives the democrats their relevance and justification for taking the paternal role which I just described. It is that ideology which is making things far worse in America."

"Yeah, but I couldn't provide for my girlfriend and my two children. I just couldn't do it on my own, and so I sold drugs to pay the bills, and that is how I ended up here."

Many in the group nodded their heads as if to say their situation was very similar, too.

It was not the first time which I had heard that recurring story. They could, if they wanted, break that cycle if someone taught them how.

"Do you want to break that cycle?" I asked.

They all nodded.

"You all want the government to leave you alone, right? You want to find productive work and to be able to provide for your children, right? You want to prove that you are not pathetic and inept like the democrats believe you are, right? You are not pathetic, right?"

"Right!" All concurred.

"The key is to adhere to those principles that create a strong, permanent nuclear family. I have been married for 26 years. My parents have been married for over 50 years. I think I speak with some moral authority on this subject. A couple's relationship starts off on the right foot by marrying BEFORE they have children (**FIRST PRINCIPLE**).

"They then bring *The Higher Power* into their relationship so that their relationship is blessed, strengthened, and guided. They pray together. 'In God They Trust' (**SECOND PRINCIPLE**). When they bring God into their marriage, new unexpected opportunities begin to appear. 'Luck,' as so many call it, starts to pop up here and there. In reality, that 'luck' is answered prayers, blessings from Heaven. Other people, such as potential employers/clients, see confidence, radiant light, wholesomeness, and a solid work ethic beaming from the couple. The couple obeys the two fundamental rules of living in a free society: (1) they do all they agree to do, and (2) they never encroach on other people's property or person (**THIRD PRINCIPLE**).

"Accordingly, people want to be around the couple. People feel they can trust them, and people bring the couple into their circles of trust.

"The couple's blessings begin to multiply, and they begin to prosper and to gain stature in their community. The husband and wife, together, teach their children those same principles (**FOURTH PRINCIPLE - TEACH THE PRINCIPLES TO YOUR CHILDREN**).

"When what I have explained is understood and lived, there is little need for a government because the family IS the government in their lives. It is what democrats fear the most...self-governance."

One inmate said, "That is exactly the life I want. But, I could never pray with my girlfriend. It would be too weird. It would be too uncomfortable."

"Praying together can feel really weird and uncomfortable at first, but it is no different from a myriad of other proper things to do. For example, some feel uncomfortable going to college, but they should go anyway. Others find it difficult to refrain from foul language, or alcohol and drugs, but they should refrain anyway. Others have a difficult time developing a solid 'worth ethic,' maintaining a clean home, clean clothes, and more. But a couple should do those things if they want the government to stay out of their life. Remember, self-governance."

"Are you saying that the democrats want us to fail so that they can become our so-called surrogate 'parent?'"

"Well, they will never admit that they want you to fail. If Americans reject the notion that government is more important than family, as the democrats believe, then the democrats will become irrelevant. So, in essence, yes. The democrats NEED you to fail so that you will NEED them. Give some deep thought to what you believe politically. What is right for you and your family?"

A few days after this political conversation, Annette informed me that our Senators were successful in their efforts to have me re-designated to FCI Englewood, Colorado.

Chapter 4

A December 2017 message written by Matthew D. Hutcheson to family and friends while at FCI - Englewood, Colorado about how Congress makes laws. Very few inmates knew the process when Matthew shared it with them. These concepts are what every American should understand about how government works.

Update December 17, 2017

How American Laws Are Made

Dear Fam,

There is something I want to share with you about the legislative process.

Right now, the United States Congress (Congress = the House of Representatives and the Senate. Together, they comprise "the Congress") is preparing to finalize a tax bill to bring to the President for his signature.

Because I am being asked so many questions every day about how the process works, I thought that I would explain it all in another update.

The term "camera" means "chamber." Old cameras had a chamber in which the film or plate was kept. The film/plate is what captured the image which came through the lens. The chamber "captures" the information to be saved/stored/remembered.

In law, the term "in camera" means "in the judge's chambers." It means something filed with the court "in camera" will be viewed by the judge while he in his chambers, and it is not shared with the public nor is it accessible on the docket. In modern terminology, it means a document is "sealed."

In legislation, there are two "chambers" of Congress, the House of Representatives and the Senate. Therefore, there are two "cameras" in which legislation is developed and viewed. The two-chamber-legislation form of government is called bicameralism. Bi, means two. Camera means chamber. So, we have a two-chamber system of law making.

What happens during the bicameral process is very interesting and I have participated in it first-hand.

A member of one chamber "drops" a Bill. Decades ago, a paper copy was literally dropped in an old oak box in the capitol building.

The clerk of either the House or the Senate would unlock the box, take all the Bills out, and register them in the legislative log. That practice of "Dropping a Bill" still happens today, but it is more ceremonial to keep the tradition alive. Bills today are sent to the clerk electronically.

The Bill is assigned to a congressional committee in which it is debated, edited, improved, etc. Then, the committee votes. If it passes committee, the Bill is presented to the leadership of the chamber.

Today, in the House, the leader is Paul Ryan from Wisconsin. Today, in the Senate, the leader is Mitch McConnell from Kentucky, both Republicans.

The leader of the chamber will decide whether to take the Bill to the entire chamber for a vote.

If it happens, and the chamber adopts the Bill, it is taken to the other chamber for its approval.

Sometimes the other chamber will simply adopt the Bill of its counterpart in "as-is" form. Then it goes to the President for signature.

However, in many instances, such as what is happening now with the Tax Bill, each chamber adopted (voted for) its own version. When it occurs that way, the differences between the two Bills must be reconciled. Reconciliation happens in something called "conference."

When a Bill goes to conference, all of the provisions of both Bills are "laid out on the table."

Those provisions upon which both chambers agree are set aside as "given" or "presumed adopted." The remaining provisions are those which contain disparities (differences) which must be discussed, and decisions made. It is "bicameralism" which comes into play.

When the United States of America came to be, bicameralism was a unique form of law making.

It ensures that laws are created for the people, by the people. When a voter calls his or her member of Congress, the voter may request a certain provision be considered in the Bill.

Those requests will at least be considered and if enough requests of a similar nature are made, the request will make it into the negotiation phase. Law makers then negotiate the differences and arrive at compromises. Sometimes it is easy. Sometimes it becomes quite heated and there are very real arguments. But eventually, a compromise is reached, and a new Bill is constructed which consists of all the original "given" provisions and all the new compromises.

Then, the new "joint Bill" is taken back to each respective chamber for another vote. If both chambers adopt the joint Bill, it is sent to the President for his consideration. If he signs it, the Bill becomes the law of the land, which is how the process works.

Life in the Extreme,

Matt

Chapter 5

Update July 4, 2018

Never, Ever, Take a Knee

Dear Fam,

I never thought I would be celebrating yet another national day of freedom without my own. But I love the United States of America and I always have. So many sacrifices have gone into making America what she is, and I want to share some heart-felt thoughts with you.

The American Revolution technically began on July 2, 1775 when George Washington took command of the continental army. General Washington was not a friend of tyranny, and King George knew that if there were any man on earth who could threaten his seat of power, it was General Washington.

The following month, on August 23, 1775, King George declared the Colonies "traitors."

The Colonists declared independence from Great Britain the following year on July 4, 1776.

The war raged on between the Colonists and Great Britain until General Cornwallis surrendered late in 1781.

France and Great Britain each recognized America's independence at the Treaty of Paris, September 3, 1783.

Even after the Treaty of Paris, things were still touch-and-go between the United States and Great Britain.

Anger and resentment still smoldered between the nations for three more decades, and eventually, war ignited again in 1812.

In the years leading up to 1812, Great Britain had captured and imprisoned over 4000 U.S. sailors. Great Britain also continued to arm American Indians with weapons and those Indians raided the Western border of the United States, causing chaos and death.

British ships harassed American trade ships at sea. Accordingly, by 1810, the United States had had enough. It stopped all commerce with Great Britain and the lack of commerce was the final spark that ignited the war on June 18, 1812.

The war of 1812 became so ugly that by 1814 the British had burned down the U.S. Capitol and the White House.

The Maryland militia rose up, with awe-inspiring bravery, and stopped the British from advancing further on land.

For a short time, the war seemed to abate, but only because Great Britain intended to finally crush the United States once and for all through a sea-to-land assault from Britain's war ships, which had been summoned and would be arriving to the place of attack within hours.

U.S. leadership asked an attorney from Baltimore, Maryland, to meet with the Admiral of the British fleet, to negotiate the release of U.S. prisoners of war being held in the belly of dozens of British war ships anchored in or near the harbor.

The young attorney boarded a rowboat and went out to meet the Admiral on board the flagship.

Once on board, the Admiral told this young attorney, whose name was Francis Scott Key, that they could negotiate, but by morning it would be pointless because most of the British fleet would arrive in hours to ultimately destroy Fort McHenry and seize control over the United States of America, once again bringing her under British rule. In other words, releasing the prisoners would happen anyway because the next day they would be British subjects.

The Admiral kept Mr. Key on board the ship to witness the frightening, dreadful appearance of dozens more British warships joining the others in preparation for delivering the final blow over Fort McHenry and the Americans.

Mr. Key went down into the belly of the ship, in which hundreds of prisoners sat chained to the hull. He described to them what it was...the final battle, and perhaps the end of the United States of America.

When darkness came, the cannons began, in sudden thunderous roar, to blanket Fort McHenry in death and destruction. For hours and hours, night's blackness was lit with the fiery explosions of cannon propelled bombs.

There was no abatement. It went on and on and on. Mr. Key could, with his own eyes aided by the light of each explosion, see that the American flag still flew over Ft. McHenry.

Through the night, the prisoners frequently inquired above, "Mr. Key, does our Star-Spangled Banner still wave?"

He yelled down into the dark prison below, "It is still there!" The prisoners erupted with the hope-inspired cheers of patriots!

The unrelenting and violent barrage lasted all night. Fort McHenry and the immediate area in which the flag flew took direct hit after direct hit. Hundreds of brave Americans died making sure that that magnificent symbol of Liberty never faltered or fell by propping it up by any means of support, knowing that by doing so, they would likely die.

They knew that if the flag fell once to the ground, the Brits would claim victorious dominion over America.

Chapter 6

THE AMERICAN FLAG MUST NOT FALL!

The patriots would give all to preserve liberty, as symbolized by the American flag.

There was no taking a knee in that gloriously heroic moment. There were only great demonstrations of courage that honored past sacrifices of their forefathers and protected America's promises for their future posterity.

Then morning came and the cannons stopped.

Once again, the prisoners shackled below inquired of Mr. Key:

Please tell us, Mr. Key

Now that the day is dawning, what do you see?

What of America's symbol of liberty?

It was there yesterday morning.

Does it still fly in majesty

After the entire night's bomb storming?

Did our symbol of hope;

Its broad stripes and bright stars

Endure and repel the encroach

Upon life, liberty and happiness' meaning?

Yes boys! Yes! It survived the reproach!

Oh how I wish you could see...it is gallantly streaming!

Take us home from this wretched blight!

The prisoners proclaimed to Mr. Key

To honor those who bravely died last night

To forever live in the land of the free. (© 2018-2020 Matthew D. Hutcheson.)

God Bless the United States of America! God Bless our beloved Stars and Stripes! God bless the loyal brave who call America home!

(Always remember, even now, that I am more free and have more rights, than most of the Pre-Revolution Colonists! Think about that the next time you see someone take a knee!)

Life in the Extreme,

Matt

Epilogue

The following was written sometime in late April or early May 2016 in a journal entry "Update" as Matthew calls them. It memorializes his experience leaving FCI-Terminal Island after five long months in solitary confinement, his transfer to USP-Victorville, and then to USP-Phoenix. Frequent transfers, such as what Matthew experienced, are called "diesel therapy" by inmates, which are long periods of time on a bus, going from prison to prison. It is cruel and unusual punishment. But note Matthew's good attitude that permeates this update. Most importantly, carefully read the goose bump-inducing story towards the end about "America! You're Still the One."

In March 2016, the prison bus transported us from FCI-Terminal Island to USP-Victorville. The drive seemed to take around two hours, but it could have been three. When we pulled into the Victorville complex, one of the inmates shouted, "Welcome to VICTIMVILLE, the most dangerous prison in America." I do not know if it is actually true, but Victorville was certainly the most intimidating place I had ever been. It was ominously frightening.

Victorville consists of a United States Penitentiary (USP), two Medium facilities, and one camp for women. After unloading my bunkie from Terminal Island at one of the Medium facilities, the bus took the rest of us to the USP. We were unloaded from the bus and walked (shackled) into a massive cement hallway that seemed to go on forever and ever.

Eventually we made it to R&D where we were unshackled. We were processed (new photo, new clothes, and interviewed), and placed in a holding tank. We were given another box lunch of peanut butter and jelly. After an hour we were escorted to the unit.

Inside the USP looks exactly what you see on TV with two cement tiers, 6x9 cells with solid metal doors with a food slot, a common eating area with a single TV, etc. Inmates can stay in the common area until 3:00 PM Monday through Friday. It is SHU-like lockdown on the weekends.

We received no actual meal that day, just two peanut butter and jelly "box lunches." I put sheets on my mattress (if it can be called that) and fell asleep exhausted. I suddenly awakened, startled, to that ever-frightening sound of keys tapping a metal door. I jumped up to see the guards yelling at me for having been asleep during the evening count. After they moved on, I lay back down and tried to go back to sleep.

The following morning around 8 AM, the cell door was unlocked. All inmates exited their cells for breakfast. In total, there were about 30-40 inmates in the unit. Breakfast was cereal and a piece of fruit. Then we were given "leisure" clothes, which consisted of blaze orange shorts and shirts.

Hygiene was also provided, and I headed straight to the shower so I could shave. We were given as much time as needed in the showers, which was the most amazing thing after having been restricted to 3 showers per week in solitary. (In solitary, we were given a 10-minute long cold shower every Monday, Wednesday, and Friday. Sometimes showers were warm if we were lucky, and no showers on the weekends. The razors were barely effective on purpose.)

Just being able to take a 15-minute shower (or longer), and to have a really close shave made me feel as though I had been liberated. Strange...it is all about perspective, is it not?

I called Annette many times a day. I cannot describe what it was like to hear her voice after having been deprived of it for so many months.

It was like coming back to life.

I was permitted to walk the USP yard. It was quite intimidating. There were guard towers everywhere with guards holding guns. Terminal Island had guard towers, too, but the guards were never seen actually holding guns. The Victorville towers are tall and ominous with real prison towers with guards just "itching."

The first day I walked the yard, I noticed my feet and ankles hurt terribly. "It is just from being cooped up for so long," I thought. "Walk it off. It will be ok." But the pain grew worse, and worse, and worse. It was not "normal" pain, and something was definitely wrong with my feet and ankles.

On the bottom tier of the unit, there is a large green door that opens to the yard. It is where all food/garbage carts come and go. After a week or two at the Victorville USP (April 2016), I was on the phone with Mom and Dad. That green door was open. I think garbage was being taken out. Suddenly I heard a loud "crack" that sounded like a cracking whip.

Moments later alarms went off and all inmates were corralled into their cells and locked down for the next week. No phone calls. No sunshine. Real lock down that lasted 5 full days. Similar to solitary but worse; no showers.

One of the guards informed us that someone had taken a hostage on the yard (the same yard I had been walking) and when the inmate did not respond to commands from the guard tower, the hostage-taker was shot and killed. It really shook me up.

In mid-April 2016, at 4:00 AM, I was notified that I would be leaving Victorville.

Around 20 inmates and I were led back to R&D, where we were given a new set of clothes (khaki elastic band waist pants) and a white T-shirt. Then, we were shackled hand and foot, and led to an awaiting bus for a long ride.

It was still dark when we boarded the bus and left the USP compound. It stopped at the Victorville Medium facilities to pick up more outgoing inmates. While waiting, the sun began to rise. Beautiful! I had not seen a sunrise in over six months.

We were on the freeway by 7 AM.

The guards piped radio music into the bus.

Country music.

We drove down the canyon, through San Bernardino, and towards Palm Springs. We were heading towards Arizona.

The sun shone through the window on my face.

The warmth soothed me, and I dozed off and began to dream.

In my dream I was on a stage with Annette and many of you. Annette and I were holding hands above our heads while waving with our other hands. Our children and other friends and family were doing likewise. Confetti and balloons rained down. Thousands of people of every race and culture were in the audience clapping, waving, and some were crying.

The audience cheered loudly and waved American flags. Loud music filled the large auditorium or stadium. The song was Shania Twain's, "You're Still the One," but slightly altered to mean "**America**, You're Still the One."

Thousands of Red, White, and Blue signs were raised by the audience. "***AMERICA! YOU'RE STILL THE ONE!***"

Then, "the knowledge was suddenly in me" (as Annette so eloquently puts it) that sometime in the future our nation will be torn asunder, from within, by a very real cultural war. Racial divisions will grow to crisis levels leaving blood in the streets and destabilizing communities. Cultural-political divisions will rise to a level in which our beautiful America will be in real jeopardy. If those divisions are not reversed, only devastating consequences awaited.

In my dream, some unknown/unseen voice said to me, "You have been chosen to heal and unite America. You were not sent to prison for something you did. You were sent for something you are going to do. You were chosen to end racial and political strife. Only someone who has been to prison AND still deeply loves America will have the credibility with the masses to unite all American people."

The Shania Twain song continued...

AMERICA!...YOU'RE STILL THE ONE!

Looks like she made it

Look how far she's come, my baby

We knew America'd get there someday

They said, we bet America'll never make it

But just look at her holding on

America's still together, still holding strong

AMERICA!...YOU'RE STILL THE ONE!

You're still the one we run to

The one that we belong to

You're still the one we want for life

AMERICA!...STILL THE ONE!

AMERICA! YOU'RE STILL THE ONE THAT WE LOVE!

The only one we dream of

AMERICA! Ain't nothin' better

AMERICA beat the odds together

We're glad we didn't listen

Look at what we would be missin'!

Bus movement jostled me out of the dream, and I straightened up astonished, shackled, and noticed country music was still playing. The dream coaxed a sobering, "whoa!" out of me.

About three hours later we pulled into FCC Phoenix, a medium security federal prison.

AUTHOR

Matthew D. Hutcheson advocates for those who do not have a voice. His advocacy favorably impacts the lives of over seventy million Americans, including investment transparency, prison reform, race relations, jobs creation in struggling economies, affordable health care access, and uniting those of varying cultures, religions, and political persuasions. A Seattle native, he is blessed with a beautiful wife and four children.

AreULost Press
For more information:
info@areulost.org

Psalm 82: 3-4

Defend the weak and the fatherless;
uphold the cause of the poor and the oppressed.
Rescue the weak and the needy;
deliver them from the hand of the wicked.

***

Other titles at **AreULost** Press available at Amazon:

Patriot in Prison Series

Quinny by Matt Hutcheson

Capitalism vs. Socialism by Matt Hutcheson

At Worshiper Warrior

Worshipper Warrior by Steve Holt (Under Worshiper Warrior Press)

God Wild Marriage – 2nd Edition by Steve Holt (Under Worshiper Warrior Press)

Other Books

Little Lamb by Jan Inman

Circle of Deception

Perspicacity: Book 3 of the Culling

Walking at the Top of the World: Book 2 of the Culling

Black Gladius: Book 1 of the Culling

Canticle of the Magios